The Punished Wound

Palewell Press

The Punished Wound

Poems – Simon Lichman

The Punished Wound

First edition 2023 from Palewell Press,
www.palewellpress.co.uk

Printed and bound in the UK

ISBN 978-1-911587-71-2

All Rights Reserved. Copyright © 2023 Simon Lichman. No part of this publication may be reproduced or transmitted in any form or by any means, without permission in writing from the author. The right of Simon Lichman to be identified as the author of this work has been asserted by him in accordance with the Copyright, Designs and Patents Act 1988

The cover design is Copyright © 2023 Camilla Reeve

The cover image – a *View of the Jerusalem Hills* – is Copyright © 2023 Derek Stein, https://derekstein-art.com/gallery/

The back cover photo of Simon Lichman by Natania Rosenfeld is Copyright © 2023 Simon Lichman

A CIP catalogue record for this title is available from the British Library.

Acknowledgements

The title of this book *The Punished Wound* is, in part, a homage to Dennis Silk's image of a '*punished land*' and to the way he welcomed me into the idiosyncratic sanctuary of his vision.
The cover painting, by Derek Stein, captures the ethereal beauty of this landscape through texture and light. Derek's intellect, understanding of construct, sense of music and words, made him an honest and trusted reader. Above all, he was a deep friend.

Over the years I have been inspired by the generous listening of:
Ron Price whose friendship blossomed through sharing poetry, becoming as sturdy as Memphis Pecans and English Oaks;
Amy Shuman and Ana Cara for endless close, creative and joyous collaboration and for arranging poetry readings;
and such dear friends as Ginette Sullivan, Gabriel Levin, Isaac Benabu, Baruch Hochman, Shlomith Rimmon-Kenan, Barbara Rosenstein, Avigail Neubach, Steve Solomons, Jonathan Wittenberg, Kate Irving, Sally-Ann Bowman, KB Nemcosky, Natania Rosenfeld, Neil Blackadder, Riva Rubin and Karen Alkalay-Gut (of the Israel Association of Writers in English), Steve Zeitlin, Amanda Dargan, Henry Abramovitch, Aloma Halter, Betsy Rosenberg, Ammiel Alcalay, Jay Shir and the South Jerusalem Tottenham Hotspur Supporters Club.
Significant steps along the way have been taken with:
Simon Freeman; John Fisher; Richard Melzack; Sarah Lichfield; Anne Freeman; Jeremy Freeman; Helena Usiskin; Kobi Freund; Avi Hofman; Roland Rance; Roslyn Herscovitz; Debbie Weinberg; Arline and Zalie Miller; Gideon Miller; and Ben Yishai Danieli. Mahadiya Barhum and Mohammed Ahmed Abdullah (Abu Yunis) and their families have been beacons of fragile hope.

Finally, I thank Camilla Reeve for her true ear, visionary editing and kindness.

Some of these poems have appeared in arc, Ariel, Ars Interpres, European Judaism, Snatched Days, Stand and TriQuarterly.

Dedication

To Rivanna, my partner in every way, whose childhood was filled with the same poetry, stories and theatre as my own childhood on a different continent, as if in preparation for spending our lives together within this challenging landscape, balancing practicality and whimsy while bringing up our children and working professionally within an atmosphere of *tikkun olam*.

To our children, Celli, Mika and Gabriella, whose clear, creative, strong, singular and independent voices bring energy and hope.

To my parents Norma and Joe, my sister Kathy and her children, Shooky, Saul and Tally, for being themselves.

And to my late brother-in-law, Dovis Miller, for his gifts of language, song and passion for justice.

Contents

Introduction 1
Twilight 5
PART 1 Liberty Peeling in the Sun 7
    Leaving the Old World 8
    Leaving London 9
    brought by dream through desert 10
    Collections Begin 11
    Finding Them as They Were My Journal 12
PART 2 Making Way 13
    Widening Roads and Cityscapes 14
    On the Road to Ramle 16
    Florence Day 17
    On Cold Days Latrun Nestles in its Firs 18
PART 3 Punishing Ourselves 19
    When Cold Wars Thaw 20
    Hour of the Just Watch 21
    Flawless 22
    of dreams and children 23
    Beyond the firs and fountain 24
    Across Gehenna 27
    Towards Kiryat Yovel 28
    Beit Safafa 29
    At the Russian Compound 30
    Arthritic Beads 31
    Orientation 32

It is good to contemplate birthdays	33
How in my heart the news	34
Wellington Boots	35
Miracle Enough	36
Route 317	37
Jerusalem Day: Mount Scopus	38
Flat Iron Flood	39
While you were making weddings	40
For Benaya	41
Four Little Boxes	42
Perspective	43
Shalom	44
Homecoming	45
Translation	46
Village School	47
East Monsoon	48
Demonstration	50
Although I have these days	51
Inheriting The Earth: Over Ireland	52
While New Jersey sleeps	53
Smothered prayer	54
Auden's Dog	55
Heat	56
June – November 2006	57
Despondency	59
July – August 2014	60

No Full Stops 61
After These Summers What More is There to Say? 62
My Children 63
PART 4 The Fragmented Weight of Wanting 65
Unatoned 66
Garden Ruminations 68
Threads 70
Backwards/Forwards 73
Twilight Barricades 74
END NOTES 75
BIOGRAPHY – SIMON LICHMAN 85

Introduction

From an early age, poetry was foremost in the why and how of my being. The gift of having to respond to a call made me seeing and seen, centred and centring, within the vibrancy of life. At first I would make up and tell stories. Later I would write as if painting, in a whirlwind of thought and emotion, accustomed to searing focus and disorientation from the intensity of *bringing through*, the concentration required to hold the world at bay, to get the aural and visual images down as entirely as possible.

My sister and I grew up in the bicultural environment of a traditional Jewish home on the outskirts of London, that was filled with paintings and books in Hebrew and English. Both parents told stories: our father, a chartered accountant, through the numbers with which he worked; our mother, an artist, through her oil paintings. We went to synagogue on Saturday mornings, to football or to our grandmother's house on Saturday afternoons, to woodlands and waterways for Sunday afternoon rambles, and to beaches in Britain and Europe for summer holidays.

Whenever the family gathered for celebrations, festivals or afternoon teas, my grandparents, parents, aunts, uncles and adult cousins would inevitably begin telling tales about the often absurd situations in which our larger-than-life immigrant ancestors found themselves as they navigated their new surroundings. Drawn to the interplay of hardship, tragedy, transcendence and humour, enacted in these chaotic storytelling exchanges through each teller's distinctive voice and style, I imbibed who we are as a family, how we arrived at each generation's 'today', via sequences of events and moments recognised as central motifs within the tapestried fabric of this dynamic journey.

My path led to studying for a B.A. in Jerusalem and falling in love with this timeless city which became my home, though I never lost my Englishness nor the sense of belonging to Britain. At university I discovered the study of Folklore, which, given my love for stories and ease with multiculturalism, was the perfect choice of academic discipline and profession.

Living in the Middle East, one is aware of the ebb and flow of populations (individuals, communities, nations and empires) which have left imprints of their cultures on the physical and spiritual landscapes, manifested in civilisation built upon civilisation, and the jostling, interwoven belief structures of Judaism, Christianity and Islam. Many of the violent conflicts that have evolved over years between the different peoples of this area, and, at times between factions within their own communities, continue to be unresolved.

For folklorists considering complex histories, the search for 'truth' lies not only in discovering and recording 'facts', but in how these facts emerge and exist within the *stories* told by those who lived them. They might track how experiences recounted within the aesthetic of a community's storytelling traditions enable generations to reflect upon the evolution of their cultural and physical environment (*facts*), how and why this process occurred (*perspective*), while transmitting networks of perception as unarticulated guidelines for shaping the future.

Were I to undertake a folkloric analysis of life within the Israeli-Palestinian conflict, in order to present the diverse communities and their 'truths', I would compare versions of the relevant stories within each community's oral tradition, examining how the narratives themselves and the individual tellers' points of view differ from, reinforce, undermine or contest each other. However, rather than an academic analysis, I found myself responding to the intellectual and emotional complexities through writing poetry and teaching.

In 1982 I began lecturing at Ben-Gurion University of the Negev, in Beersheba, Israel, which has a mixed Bedouin and Jewish student population. These students had little contact with each other outside of class, and mostly felt uncomfortable together as they were troubled by fear and ignorance of different cultures and religious beliefs. Using the sensibilities underlying folklore fieldwork and scholarship in my approach to education, I encouraged students to include aspects of their family folklore and the challenges experienced in daily life during class discussions of academic subjects such as Folklore, Literature or Theatre studies. The students gradually relaxed in what became a more enriching learning environment.

These interactions introduced me to multifaceted perceptions of history, held by various Jewish and Arab communities in Israel, and highlighted some of the difficult social, economic, political and educational issues facing them. I realised that I wanted to focus on education that would contribute to the strengthening of our 'Shared Society' and in 1991, I established *The Centre for Creativity in Education and Cultural Heritage* (*CCECH*) (a non-governmental organisation), in order to bring together Arab and Jewish children, parents, grandparents, teachers and principals through school-community pairing programmes and college courses, based on folklore.

In the Jewish and Arab school-pairing programmes, pairs of classes work together over a period of two years. Children research their own folklore, collecting information from their families. The children meet in Joint Activities, designed around parents and grandparents in their capacity as tradition-bearers and folk artists, where they explore both communities' traditions of, for example, play, foodways, religious practices and family stories. The teacher training and enrichment programmes provide a forum in which students can examine stereotypes they have of each other and of themselves, while learning how the rich cultural resources of their own families can be used in multicultural and shared-society education.

Through this work I have been immersed in a plethora of narratives and privy to fears, frustrations and hopes of individuals and communities which, together with my own background and experiences, are the inspiration for these poems.

The Punished Wound is a personal landscape within a seemingly unresolvable conflict - a wound, suffered by us all, which can only be healed by us all.

Simon Lichman

References to Biblical stories, literature, dates and geographic locations can be found in endnotes. There is no glossary of events, current or past, since *facts, definitions, explanations* or *maps*, in conflict situations, are not free from the perceptions of myriad interest groups and contentious connotations and are subject to debate and heated argument. For readers interested in the history of this area and how the conflict (referred to in Hebrew as, 'The Situation') evolved, there is a wealth of easily available source materials and academic discussions covering varying points of view.

Twilight

*Compare night jasmine
to half-scent rose and buddleia
mixed with milk light everlasting
lamb bleat and cow call
close fit corn
chestnut fade to copper beech
fox and fieldmouse
start across their zigzag
as if we wait for something else
to pattern pastel sky quilt of land
farmhouse in its tuck of hillside
blackbird flight to hawthorn
a velvet hunter's gun
vermillion night has come.*

PART 1
Liberty Peeling in the Sun

Leaving the Old World

From a pilgrim's journal
Years on. How many saw the yachting on the Hudson? How many carved so deep that what remained was space into which we dreamed we'd pour our souls. We fled on boats called 'The Mayflower' and 'The Glory', 'The Golden Ladies' and 'The Arm of Liberty.' I hear you calling "Liberty, what crimes" (what crimes?) "committed in your name" (what were their names?).

    Light between the rafters and the rails.
    No hint of flower
    whistles through this dug-out rock.
    The arm waves full of hollow sunlight
    (From France, they came, "Join us.")

    Sweet corn sunk through fishponds
    Rotted cars and cable reels
    Besuited men beside their polished steel
    Spade-to-hands beneath the open skies.

    I'd never seen those New York days.
    The misbegotten
    eye their wait into my nights.
    *(I must not sleep
    if the shoes fit and they're mine.)*
    Manhattan Wharves
    (Keep candles bright)
    Not brave Nor indigo
    Call the ships to harbour

    Desert for gold.

Leaving London

From an evacuee's notebook
We were sent by train – they said it was a Sunday

Bricked up windows gaswork frames
(Kings Cross Euston Waterloo)
Tunnel tracks pull chimney stacks
Deep lawns and allotments.
Caravans in the wrong dream of light

Pigeon hawk copse spinney
Crystal starlings' sweep of water
The undone in a suitcase
Shaved heads and punctured eyes.

We glide through ghosted Duffield
Colours fade houses slide
The roots no longer hold.

At devil's wrench of Chesterfield
Wind fits into rung of spine
Ebony scaffolds crows in rain
Mauve green off-white white
Forget their names.

Sheffield is the last stop
I polish shoes in the aisles of this train.

brought by dream through desert

It was the only beast we found
silk scarves unwound at corners in the wind
belongings crowd the eye of home
hands fumbling.

They were broken, the brothers
the lost ears of summer
worn mislaid and quiet
heavy in the roots.

Fetch wood
Thresh wheat
Grind between rough stone
Brick out ovens of clay.
Smoke troubles the birds of prey.
Trace maps upon our bread.
Eat it down.
Let Phoenicia burn.

It is my heart. It is our gold.

Collections Begin

from K's Book
With love from D

Glass beads that caught her fancy
scarves thrown out for rags
battered between secret covers.
Hope, she called, *were I to see your face*
I would no longer care
for I'd be flying home no matter where
that light would draw me.
Draw me.

When she left the boat
we watched until the edge of sight
leaving one on guard
so she'd be welcomed on return.
By the time we had the hatch off
and were in the sea
only the wood remained -
she had grown weary of the weight.

Finding Them as They Were
My Journal

From "Elvira Shetayev's Diary"
We will not live / to settle for less
We have dreamed of this / all our lives

Do not ask for hope.
Do not ask.
There should be threads running through.
There should be golden runnings.
We are alone they cried
in the wind before the nights broke
no-one followed they thought
fingers carving icecap
you could see they spoke
breath through crumbled skull
what wandered heart to heart
pity hope dying thus
and in each other's arms
they cannot last
driven from within by our imagining.

PART 2
Making Way

Widening Roads and Cityscapes
Old Trees Get Lonesome

1

Rounding the bend you see a row of sturdy carob
and some spreading eucalyptus
we should remember them as they are today
large and bountiful, flowing with almost chocolate
and a scent that almost clears the head.
We should remember them mighty in their grasp of soil
Samson grown and seemingly invincible.

Once upon a time a poor woodcutter
lived in the forest with his axe
and the axe begat the buzz-saw
which begat the bulldozer
which begat the men who told the bulldozers
where to go (who were not foresters)
who plotted against the sweep of hill
and these deep-rooted trees.

2

or gash a bypass
through verdant hills
uproot the rock
ignore the sculptured terrace
being careful only with the pylons
all the rubbish buried deep
for where cars play it does instead of seed

3

What do they do
with the fine stone
set in its place
all those years ago
by the gentle hands
of stone masons -
do they number them
sell them off in auctions
thread them into necklaces of
honour for the heavy weights of
policy who determine what our children's
children will collect for their museums
as evidence of a world
in which they could have lived?

4

so
cut into
that it cannot fold
from stone age into iron
cannot say
roll your hand
over these my ups and downs
for nothing will endure
our rifling days –
in this plasticine age
it seems we mould the land into
models of our sharp-edged selves.

On the Road to Ramle

i

Kneeling in the dust of grace
these dancing pears
raise fuchsia arms
to catch a space of light.

ii

Wagtails sift rain-turned earth for seed
the oval moon askance watches
an apricot of gold ease herself
from the skies.

iii

An awkward strut of quail
through green wash of clay
too soft for giant steps.

iv

Hands of leaf offered in the sun
towards Latrun our eyes run.

Florence Day

Russet leaves dragged windwise
across terracotta roofs.
Rafael shafts of light sweep
Ghirlandio greens into the west.
You can just see God settling
these imported pines down for the night.

On Cold Days Latrun Nestles in its Firs

That is to say I have seen the sun
glance off the edges of these fields
where the unusual heaviness of snow stands
technicolour shoots out from the solid clay.
Mist drops to fill a corridor of alcoves
with the changing shape of heaven.
I can believe in Paradise
to have witnessed light such as this
until the next car bursts by
the next hand casts its first stone.

PART 3
Punishing Ourselves

When Cold Wars Thaw

Superkiss opened the icebox
long enough for the thaw to overtake the world
which is a small place nowadays.
And as the Mississippi overran its course
Euphrates swelled and flooded Eden.

"Noah's coming,"
called the animals, "Noah's coming."
"Dummies, can't you leave your children",
I said, "two of a kind." "Oh no, not that again.
If they don't go, we don't go."

From the top of the Lincoln Memorial
Superkiss reviewed his work
calling to El Salvador in Chinese
"Yeah! It is good."

Jetlag makes you weary.

Hour of the Just Watch
Netanya, August 1982

Out here in the dead of night
time hums and cars pace
the backroads between
the war and the deep blue sea.

They tell us
the sea's polluted these days
and it reflects my heart
beating unjustifiably out of sync.

They say
the world is turning
around the wrong axis
that yesterday's sand
is tomorrow's coca-cola bottle.

I say
when the green mosaic moon has your face
I can believe we'll make it past the midnight.

Flawless
September 1982

When I see you with my dreams
ice-cream and rosewater
on constant cannon ash
I know where lies the right to examine the
deaths and loneliness forgiveness and pity who
Dylan found flawless in the flames of London.

But these unseen in our flames
before birth clearly stamped
in the eye of generations
U. S. Made   Made in Russia
made in secret tried in public
sometimes in the name
Israel Palestine Canaan
names.

I hear this land calling
ageless and lost forever
if indeed there was an ever
for us always to ignore.

# of dreams and children

But did you have a friend
a friend such as this
a friend who was ill
that you could not reach
hold out your hand
I'll take you through,
I'll take you through.

Or if you had a son
loved him
watched him grow
and he grew into Absalom
swinging you from the tree
with your hair all tangled
what would you do?
What would you do my friend?
Perhaps, if only a little,
you might lament.

I had a home once
    yours
          mine
yours
    mine

Tired land beats
the boots we wear
never winning
never losing
never leaving alone

Beyond the firs and fountain

    these views

of a sea sunk
          into its depths of salt

    pearling

        oleander, sage and oak

mountains chipped
          into the tracks of wild gazelle

a ridge of paintbrush evergreens

            carved from light
   along
       an edge of branch

within
    a thin blue sky

blown to almost chalk
         rising in the

    distant rose of Jordan.

These things I have known –

calmness as
          a crumpled edge of cuff
    shown

from maroon sleeves of a Greek jersey

          church bells tolling hours

Muezzin call and mumbled *Ma'ariv*.

These things I have seen –

a blue/red bag
          balanced as an easel on the knees
    olives

bent into their crook of sun
              stairs of handpicked stone
down to bedrock run
          single seeds of summer

spaced in sycamore clung.

                                        /continued

Small things that raise
                      small flickers in the heart.

We are the flotsam of closed borders
                            thrown up in the arms of a dying sea

we comb our separate shores
                    for trophies rustling desert attics.

Small things to be sure –

                    we cannot
stand a row of trees
                out from the light
      by saying:
              fir/blue/day

and peace is just a word.

Across Gehenna

Platinum edge of sun
four crows drift over rim of world
smidgen blue towards the vanished sea.
Someone cuts an arena into the hillside
where the houses steep towards
the healing place Augusta Victoria
spire lost in mist
the future unrevealed today.

Towards Kiryat Yovel

The humpty pearl of sun
sinks behind Jubilee Hill
red blood to pastel crescent
quick glow quickening
dusk come darkness
for there is no
unconditional half-light
where boundaries
blur into a world unseen
and we pretend electric stars
welcome us as we are.

Beit Safafa
September 2001

thrown
rose of sharon
dropping into
unpeaceful moments
thousands of miles
westward for a change
fooling us into the deep breath
of sleeping well tonight.

At the Russian Compound

The dishevelled ones
outside prison gates
quiet in their unadoring motion
shoulders raising slough of back

and the repossessed kissing
god-drenched flagstones set
into the tars of modern pine

heaven is the only thing
that openly threatens here
but the rain won't fall
from the marquetry of blue
gold blue chrome sky
waiting
waiting for the deluge.

Arthritic Beads

holding threads of life
they tease meaning
out of the quiet chink
of sacred digits
separating
this thing from the other
this name of God
from that friday prayer
or thursday afternoon
this day of hope
from all the other days
in which we worry away the rose
slipping off the frayed edge
of the order we enclose.

Orientation

Or standing
in Independence Park
back to King George Street
facing the Old City
absent mindedly noting where you are
according to contemporary blots of skyline
these in school - this one too far North for markers
the dinosaur domes and steeples defying gravity with grace
predict a settledness of day until developed or blown away.

It is good to contemplate birthdays

in this soft light briefly
turning city pink to cream sand
almost blanketing out the sound
of cannon fire in the blessèd house of bread
the roman candle of my cake
showers into Beit Sahur
where quiet Franciscans built
their Church of Shepherds' Field
to illuminate darkness –
the wind is up
as if more powerful
than the havoc at our disposal.

How in my heart the news

as I see them all but do not feel
the death watch blood clot by our door
for today my boy is ten –
the sky remains in place
the trees call with the wind's race through
and none of us knows what guns are for.

Wellington Boots

While you're away
I use your pillow to ease myself
into the buffered sleep of Christmas Eve
rain drumming sallies on car tops and
filling up the Shepherds' Fields with mud –
must be this
that slows Salvation down.

Miracle Enough

The moon almost gone
the terraces springy green
the day acting as if in place
suggests room to meander
wherever would go.

Route 317

Acrid rubbish burning
somewhere in the hills
beyond the road past Hebron
trace of sky fade grey green brown
dry walled olive groves and grapevines
were it just this calm
You come to my land I'll come to yours
amongst varied views of empty space
bound by greed books and promises
ignored unread unsaid
inconsequential and irrelevant
crushed history
calling
if not here then where?

Jerusalem Day: Mount Scopus

Muffled *Muezzin / Cohanim*
backing the fire and rumble
strange day traffic
tramping feet and armoured cars
ebb and flow of seascape sky
sounding neither lyrical nor new
in air that wafts through
catastrophe and jubilation -
it is Jeremiah grieving
beside the bones of Absalom
See how you turn the names around?

Flat Iron Flood

Because in the flat iron heart of here
lies our intention to be blessed
above all other living things
with a voice to sing and an eye to record
the way weight grinds us into dust begun

the now now now of the then then then
drumming drumming drumming
from mists of distant past
to futures refused to see

I sent you blue prints and
a basic list of what-not-to-do
I sent a Book and Another and Another
Global Warming too

arms around necks of animal and tree
taken down to breathless images you cannot free.

While you were making weddings

and we were making Purim costumes
someone somewhere close
was making bombs
to blow up buses
shopping centres
who knows what
wholeness shot to pieces
hung on a sketch of hope.

For Benaya

i

these are the fallen
not the mighty nor the good
the gorgeous nor the wise
but a chance collection of sound bits
rubbing shoulders with each other
for perhaps the only time
in this waft
unbeing
to
having just begun

ii

arms
of silhouette
towards a noon sun
edged by desert craters
wandering in the space
of whatever happened
to

Four Little Boxes
for Uri

Once upon a time there were three little foxes
Who didn't wear stockings, and they didn't wear sockses,
But they all had handkerchiefs to blow their noses,
And they kept their handkerchiefs in cardboard boxes.

They lived in the forest in three little houses,
And they didn't wear coats, and they didn't wear trousies.
They ran through the woods on their bare little tootsies,
And they played 'Touch Last' with a family of mouses.

We bury another of our children's friends
In a neat row of four little shockses,
They wear plain *tallises* and don't wear sockses,
And they play Touch Last in misled boxes.

Perspective

Bring bulldozers before dawn
(stealthily for this could raise a storm and
it is best to do these things in darkness)
begin with outward walls
moving through new rubble
to the heart of home
tooth paste hair shampoo books
loved arms of doll and teddy bear
waving from crushed windows
on the summit of our independence.

Shalom

They beat their tiny wings against my back
according to the pace of running after
to say those little things
in the words (too few) we share
Thank you, Simon – How are you, Simon?
They like to use my name
but it is not enough to stand between
what is and all that was
is not enough to keep
the roads paved and the crops intact.
Yet I will pit the promise of this name against
the gathering clouds of summer snow
that rots the roots of all we grow.

Homecoming

I love coming back to these eager faces
turned into a promise of safe schools
working limbs and straight teeth
taking us beyond borders
and negotiation.

Translation

Sitting within the
dream of being seen
they discuss
how much of this how
much of that to serve their guests
light slanting into the grey room
between branches and the dampish day
we are not locked into the vagaries
of diplomacy or hardening hearts
ignited expectation raises us into
a warmer space where we can learn
the dignity of many tongues.

Village School

for we know
this is neither a game
of hopscotch nor a jar of pickles
this addled eye and butchered soul
what do the policy makers see
in cracked stone abodes
and shredded olive tree
when they close
if they close
their eyes what do they see –
nations spilling opportunity in the
unthinking grasp of idol stores and desert beds
doves unfreed from floods gannets from oil slicks
birds of prey patrolling splintered lands
unable to separate
honey from curdled milk
flowing from affliction
dry rock from contemplation?

East Monsoon
for Imam Abdullah and Principal B

Thus the snippy snappy crocodile
with slippy slidey eyes
glides from shallow glades
to grab our legs and drag us
drowning down
as the birds sing and the
sun slants over a lagoon
airlessly asking ourselves
how come the steely jaws
still take us by
surprise.

Barracuda shoals patiently
encircling filigree hope
shining through eyes of the
otherwise despairing young
thrown into a conflict
they had not begun
that shreds the flesh of future
from their supple bones?

Yet they look at you with
the intensity of fresh love
leavened by equality
and you want to say
It will always be this way
holiest of holies echoing
how do we make justice stay
do we make justice stay
make justice stay
make justice
justice
stay

Demonstration
4th November, 1995

exploded organ emptying on the roadmap
of how did we get from there to here
how within this cauldron
of hope against heartlessness
do we patch a ragged shape
for blood to course around
its proper place?

Although I have these days

when brightness is too high
but how easy it might have been
to guide fragments into harmony
complete this unsure dance
with the imperfect steps of Eden.

Inheriting The Earth: Over Ireland

From up here the roads look deserted
the cars too small to see
the fields crocheted around copses
and clumps of refracted light.

It makes the dwellings
look inviting and perhaps they are -
Wren Boys out at Easter and corn dollies
dancing in their barns through winter nights.

It looks like butter
wouldn't melt in its mouth
and yet it is no different
from our own land
seen through the clouds
people-less and waiting
for the meek.

While New Jersey sleeps

someone
stealthily mixes cocktails
sends children off
to twenty hours down a mine.

While New Jersey sleeps
I'm waiting for day
in the cradle of halloween worlds
where corpses rise from coffins
and ghouls tap window panes
wondering if the news is good
are they talking to each other
are they talking?

Do they open their lips
so that their mouths
can declare our praise?

Do they stand or kneel
for the occasion
and when their sins are listed
do they beat their chests
with fists clenched
over blinkered hearts?

Smothered prayer

fills each others' shoes
crushing balanced peace
into unfair mercies visited
upon the generations
in dismembered
consideration
compromise
understanding
consolation

Auden's Dog

They never forgot
That even the dreadful martyrdom must run its course
Anyhow in a corner, some untidy spot
Where the dogs go on with their doggy life and the
                                        torturer's horse
Scratches its innocent behind on a tree.

                  With all these deaths lying
                  around our children's eyes
                  how can we console them
                  this was chance this was ailing
                  no rhyme nor reason
                  no suitable words to say
                  no explanation
                  of how things go
                  their own sweet way?

Heat

i

They sit around and worry
about missiles everywhere
they say there is no other way
iron fist at midnight
wrecking ball by day
boys and girls fighting
without rights to nay-say
but sitting at my table
or walking my dog's way
as long as I am able
I'll talk and write today
how desolation in our midst or periphery
takes its toll upon our soul destroying you and me.

ii

Or do they call each other on hotlines:
Whoopee it's August (June or July)
let's get back to the eye for an eye
if you move Glass Goliath White Pawn 3
to threaten Black Queen Widow Judy
safe beside her Rook
we might manage weeks of warfare
before Other Nations claim deaths seen
have gone beyond 'acceptability'
if we're lucky we could cook another week or two
before a ceasefire is organised and Phew once again
we'll have avoided negotiating me and you.

June – November 2006

i

I move lead limbs around my chores
assessing the balance of blood
to see if it explains despondency -
withdrawing from the bank
posting poems to a friend.

What has finally broken
through the old defense of
hurtling into work and play?
This one in his tin can
or that footless bandaged boy
this sense of one more
one more time
until we use up all the people
before the waters end
and we return
to spears and sling shots?

ii

*But these are children
held and vanished
old and fresh
blunted
as they move from
school to war
to night-shaken
day-lit ghosts
of all things passed.*

iii

Broken hill wasted *wadi*
cedars gone to flame
outrunning
sibling pines and oak
mongooses and voles
scorpions and salamanders
I have a child who counted them
for conservation – it was hard because
she couldn't tell which she'd seen before
but we can recognise these eyes and ears
count their hearts
must always know how in death
they are never told apart.

iv

for when facing this or that
what is worse than not by
cancer or sclerosis
or a peanut in the wind pipe
with no one knowing the manoeuver?

Despondency

i

Thus as the final curtain falls
on a season of Goldoni's *War*
blood flows in the Comedy of Life
(as opposed to Dell'arte)
a little joke we play on ourselves
that back pains and toothaches
crohns and migraines
are our real concerns.

ii

They talk of calling up thirty thousand
not to build hospitals or replant woodland
but to soldier forth against
who knows how few
as kill and maim they do
kill and maim we do.

iii

Clog the streets with bodies
clog the streets with fear
clog arteries with dusty battle
the air full of despair.

July – August 2014

i

Unable to travel to our Great
Niece's *Batmitzvah* in London
I write to friends and relations
At least we are safe.
For *safe* read: *alive*
for *alive* do not read:
hopeful
looking forwards
ebullient carefree.

ii

If I've written one poem
to accompany all the others
about this punished wound
let's say it is enough
enough people
do you ask?
enough poetry?

No Full Stops

So here's a page of paper
traditionally white I suppose
because black words bounce
best into meanings set -
phrase sentence comma
stops and starts
dancing life on
surfaces crisp and clean

when really I'm wondering
about another poem
describing a different scene
where bodies are the page
and sops of blood are
sentence comma phrase

After These Summers What More is There to Say?
for Dennis

They threw the world up
and we watched the pieces
spinning through the sun's light
conjuring new dimensions
with parts and patterns
they had fitted into.

But the jugglers were untried
and although as thieves they had our trust
some of us saw them winking to each other
as they slipped faceless through a closing door.

My Children

When I think of you
I realise a fragility
I'd unthought
in my slipshod way
for I can see the violent
leer of loss lick of tongue
sadness overlooked
peace overcome.

PART 4
The Fragmented Weight of Wanting

Unatoned

1

Because
we cannot see
how to defeat these
incumbent advents of ego
(not having banished any of it
though often told we help
hearts eagle owl-ways
into brighter skies)
who smoothly bully
further degradation into
their sacrilege of broken air
as if staring frozen within the
glare of raw evil we had neither
faced in action nor in prayer.

2

Remember sitting outside this house when
the cedars quaked night after night star beside star
the steady shark's heart beating without ache and
began wondering what had been visited upon spot-lit
refugees where unleashed beasts mauled and mauled?
And here we are again
as the next generation without decency or reflection disregards
what is dismantled by fire and by flood pestilence and desire
our hope is that these and these their actions will be found
wanting intellect and soul generosity and understanding -
is it not prophesied that leopards lions and wolves
shall coexist with lambs kids and calves
but manipulated fortune and ignored experience
determines which of us creates the habitat.

3

What
will I do
when they (we)
approve the next
air-struck demolition
of circus cannons
peopled lines of
stone insult and flying fire
as over every top we go
bedudgeon sound or no
to keep us hold us
beckoned by
prophetic bodies
sewn into godless ground?

4

clung how need not give in
to hatred or despair need not confound
a rise above where spirits differentiate
between the wise and wicked
wise – the one who tries to comprehend
wicked – the one who simply does not care
for in the caring we display links between
lives we could have led
and lives that need atonement
wrists conjuring dull and foul
thought into flights of fancy
landscapes we should like to see
ourselves stripped free
of ambiguity.

Garden Ruminations

1

Thus in the smallness of events
call them what they are – *annihilations*
spiritual leaders at table with their pupils
shop fronts waiting for decoration
olive groves prepared for harvest
off-to-school or reaching home blocks
ones twos becoming tens of thousands
as marauding hoards of
kitchen knives machetes machine and hand guns
pipe and cluster bombs crammed with nails
tractors motorbikes and cars
like mine like yours
rip god's image into a formless mass
unmendably whistling down winds of desolation.

2

Strangers
remain awake and
cold in camps and caravans
along silk roads and trading routes
train stations and our very doorways
Let them in Let them in I hear you say
while many turn their cheeks away
contrary to the Books of Balance
in which the land promised
a milk and honeyed flow
compassion and
crops to grow
(not bordered conquest)
causing light to glow.

3

Yet these too are our people clinging to
uncertain hilltops by the fingernails of faith
to prevent a grand slide down to earth -
what will they say
when stood on nightly palm
facing the moments of their day
how to explain
Although
Your people
hardened hearts
charted this way
in belief
the others had
gone astray?

4

Let us be strong.
Let us be firm.
Let us retain the image
while we have legs for moving
hands for holding
pencil paintbrush violin bow
unclogged brains to shape refrains
our lips could utter beyond
God willing God is great
There by the grace of God
oh let us
save ourselves
from an armageddon too large for fig
leaves to camouflage these marks of Cain.

Threads

1

Yes
you were
right my friend
the canker slipped in
well before conception yet
we had to try turning the tide
of fracture and disintegration
call us *Canute*
Stubborn and *Unschooled*
Stupid and *Inexperienced*
even call us *Dreamer*
as in this fable no one's left to
witness continental platelets disengage
meridians flatten into the detritus of our design.

2

When all I can think of is to lie in bed
watching TV or reading a gripping yarn
anything but more
of this blurred stack of people
dropped below the radar of carpets
unwound in their unraveled dive to earth
instead
I play the evergreen music of my spheres
continue faithfully recording
unmagic jumps of joy
unshared space cannot afford.

3

and in dreams search
visionary ways ahead
which step sideways
sometimes
then forge forwards
with clarity and clear flight
unlike journeys I had ever known
alone in landscapes of
foreboded loss and blotted sight

4

for even amongst the
lightlessness of babbled dream
some promised that if we lived
according to genetic codes
we could yet embody the flawed
perfection of earth's scheme.

5

We throw
our heads back
fill our lungs
open shredded sockets
shake fresh-grown hair
and pull those pillars down
free from greed and violation
be the bright ones
climbing stairs carved out
of desolation and despair
to do to dare

/continued

6

singing excavated skill to caulk
hulks bobbed beyond brink
keep eyes bright arms young
hold unhoused mariners
unbound by laws of
misused gravity

7

sunk saturated waterless
befuddled brain impaired inner strain
unable to push off from sea beds
shed tangled wait for primaeval
surge surprising upwards
take us through
return again and once again
bring another and another few
into transcendent view

8

for hope
defying proved reality
like love
is the greatest gift
with which
we have been blessed
the greatest mystery.

Backwards/Forwards

these same silver clouds
rolling grey/steel/mauve
over long loved hills
shifting light on terraces
shell-white towers
shape changing sky-lakes
offering some suggestion
that beyond it all
there might be tranquillity

and I ask this same same question
with the same same heaviness of heart
from whence cometh direction
to dissolve wills that dis-unite
dismember and delude
damage down disable
imagining flash of blue
touch of scarlet
a poem or two

for this is the story of
a more than half-lived life
struggling into an order of its own
with this one thread of reason: Making
making things
as if to say
this could be better
it will be so.

Twilight Barricades

*visited in this other scheme unable
to trace steps from river-mouths
to stream boulders to mountain top
swayed chaotic dream
shaken from myself in every way
or in reverie roaming
far from this here of pitted fear
bleached stone blunt sand
splurge of fresh grass if the rain falls
realising that all its depths of green
rolling hills bluebell dells the shy
primrose and sheltered snowdrops
would not draw me back
I wept at loss rejoiced at understanding.*

END NOTES

Acknowledgements and Dedications
The Punished Land, Dennis Silk, (Middlesex: Penguin Books, 1980).

Tikkun Olam (Hebrew: 'repairing the world').

Introduction
The following poems and essay describe the feeling of 'receiving' and writing poetry: *Song of a Man Who Has Come Through*, D.H. Lawrence, The Complete Poems, (Middlesex: Penguin Books, 1971); *Memory,* Pablo Neruda (trans. Alastair Reid), Pablo Neruda: Selected Poems, (New York: Dell Publishing, 1972); and *Play and Theory of the Duende*, Federico García Lorca, Deep Song and Other Prose, (London: Marion Boyars: 1980).

Israel has a heterogeneous education system which is divided into three streams of schools for the Hebrew speaking community (secular, religious and ultra-orthodox) and one stream for the Arabic speaking community. Most Jewish and Arab children do not have natural opportunities of meeting, apart from those who attend the few mixed-population bilingual schools.

For a description of these programmes see *Knowing Ourselves/Knowing Each Other - Traditional Creativity in the Multicultural School Setting of Israel*, in 'Folklore Studies: Past, Present - and Future?', special edition of Lore and Language, Vol. 15, Number 1-2, ed. J.S. Ryan, (University of Sheffield, 1997). For additional publications written by Simon Lichman and Rivanna Miller, see the Centre for Creativity in Education and Cultural Heritage website: ccech.org

The term 'The Situation' may be compared with 'The Troubles' of Northern Ireland.

Part 1: *Liberty Peeling in the Sun*
The Statue of Liberty was a gift to the American people from France in recognition of the Abolition of Slavery and the inspiration American Independence offered French society in the pursuit of its own democracy.

Leaving the Old World
The names of the ships carrying British Pilgrims to North America are fictitious apart from the 'Mayflower'.

Madame Roland, a revolutionary leader who fell out of favour, cried out from the scaffold before she was beheaded, *Liberty, what crimes are committed in your name?*

brought by dream through desert
The poem, in part, refers to the story of Joseph and his brothers. See Genesis 37, 39, 40-47.

Finding Them as They Were - My Journal
Quotation from *Phantasia for Elvira Shatayev*, Adrienne Rich, The Dream of a Common Language, (New York: W.W. Norton, 1978).

Widening Roads and Cityscapes
Reference to the song, *'Hello In There'*, by John Prine.
You know that old trees just grow stronger
And old rivers grow wilder every day
Old people just grow lonesome
Waiting for someone to say, 'Hello in there, hello.'

For the story of Samson, see Judges 13-16.

On the Road to Ramle
Ramle is a town in Israel lying along an ancient trading route, part of which used to be the main artery between Jerusalem and Tel Aviv.

On Cold Days Latrun Nestles in its Firs
Latrun is a Trappist monastery in the foothills of Jerusalem (built 1891-1897).

When Cold Wars Thaw
During the 1970s, Henry Kissinger travelled the globe extensively as the United States Secretary of State. A cover photograph of Newsweek in 1974, showed Henry Kissinger's head superimposed on Superman's body, which became a popular poster. For the story of Noah see Genesis 6-9.

Hour of the Just Watch & Flawless
Israel-Lebanon War, June-September 1982.

Netanya is a coastal town in northern Israel.

Ceremony after a Fire Raid, Dylan Thomas: The Poems, (London: J.M. Dent & Sons, 1978).

of dreams and children
Absalom led a revolt against his father, King David (II Samuel 15-18).

Beyond the firs and fountain
Written before the 1994 Peace Treaty between Israel and Jordan, from a vantage point above the roofs of Mishkenot Sha'ananim (a cultural centre in West Jerusalem) overlooking the Dead Sea.

The *Muezzin* calls Moslems to prayer.
Ma'ariv is the Jewish evening prayer.

Across Gehenna
The Valley of Hinnom is also known as Gehenna (Hell). According to the Armistice Agreement of 1949 which ended the Israeli War of Independence, the southern part of the valley was in Jordan, the northern part was in Israel. The view in the poem is of the middle section of the valley which was No Man's Land up to the 1967 Arab-Israeli War after which the whole valley came under the jurisdiction of Israel.

Santa Augusta Victoria is a community hospital on the Mount of Olives, East Jerusalem (built 1907-1914).

Towards Kiryat Yovel
Kiryat Yovel (Jubilee Hill) is a western suburb of Jerusalem.

Beit Safafa
Beit Safafa is a Palestinian village located in southern Jerusalem. The border between the newly formed Israel and its neighbours, determined by the 1949 Armistice Agreement and known as the Green Line, ran through Beit Safafa, leaving half the village in Jordan, the other half in Israel. After the 1967 Arab-Israeli War, both sides of the village came under the jurisdiction of Israel.

The poem was written with the 9/11 attack on the Twin Towers (New York) in mind.

At The Russian Compound
The Russian Compound in the centre of Jerusalem, includes the Holy Trinity Cathedral of the Russian Orthodox Church (built 1860-1872), a Police Station and the Moscovia Detention Centre.

Arthritic Beads
Waiting Room - Bikkur Holim Hospital, Jerusalem City Centre.

It is good to contemplate birthdays and ***Wellington Boots***
Bethlehem (House of Bread), Beit Jala and Beit Sahur are Palestinian towns located in the Occupied West Bank, south of Jerusalem. Between 2000-2002, during the Second Intifada, there were ongoing hostilities between Beit Jala and Gilo (predominatly Jewish neighbourhood southwest Jerusalem).

How in my heart the news and ***Miracle Enough*** refer to *Every True Miracle*, Susan Stewart, Yellow Stars and Ice, (Princeton: Princeton University Press, 1981).

Route 317
Route 317 is a main road running through the Occupied West Bank, from the southern outskirts of Jerusalem to Beersheba, via Hebron.

Last line refers to Rabbi Hillel (Ethics of Our Fathers 1:14)
If I am not for myself, who will be for me?
And yet when I am for myself, what am I?
And if not now, when?

Jerusalem Day: Mount Scopus
The border between Jordan and Israel (according to the Armistice Agreement of 1949) separated East and West Jerusalem. 'Jerusalem Day' marks East Jerusalem coming under the jurisdiction of Israel after the 1967 Arab-Israeli War.

The Hebrew University of Jerusalem, on Mount Scopus, overlooks the Old City of Jerusalem.

The *Cohanim* are descendants of Temple priests who retain the rôle of blessing congregations during certain prayers.

Flat Iron Flood
The poem follows the logic of a *God Will Save Me* traditional joke. There are references to: Ecclesiastes 3: 20 (*dust...to dust*);

the *Ten Commandments*, Exodus 20:1-15; the Bible (Old and New Testaments); and the Koran.

While you were making weddings
Purim celebrates the story of Esther (see Book of Esther, Old Testament). As well as reading the *megillah* (scroll) in synagogue, festivities take place within a carnival atmosphere of dressing up in costumes and lighthearted misrule.

For Benaya
Benaya Zuckerman (1986-2004) was killed on his way to school in a bus bombing, Jerusalem.

Four Little Boxes
Uri Grossman (1985-2006) was killed in combat, Israel-Lebanon War.

Quotation from, *The Three Foxes*, When We Were Very Young, A.A. Milne, (London: Methuen, 1924).

Tallises are Jewish prayer shawls. (English variation of the Yiddish *Talleisim*, based on the Hebrew: *talit;* pl. *talitot*).

Perspective / Shalom / Homecoming / Translation / East Monsoon / Village School
were written in, or about, some of the communities which have participated in CCECH's shared-society folklore programmes bringing together Jewish and Arab Moslem and Christian school children, families and teachers.

Jewish children in the diaspora are given Hebrew names as well as names from the country in which they are living. In 1950s Britain, children called *Shalom* were usually named Steven or Simon.

The Holy of Holies was the inner sanctum of the Temple. The High Priest, the only person with the mandate to enter, would pray there exclusively on The Day of Atonement.

Demonstration
Assassination of Israeli Prime Minister, Yitzhak Rabin, 1994.

Reference is made to Hope Against Hope: A Memoir, Nadezhda Mandelstam, (New York: Atheneum Books, 1970).

Inheriting the Earth: Over Ireland
The Wren Boys perform traditional Irish mumming plays or folk dramas. Some agricultural communities fashion a 'corn dolly' out of the last sheaf of corn and place it over the threshold of the barn to assure the success of next year's harvest.

Blessed are the meek, for they shall inherit the earth,
Sermon on the Mount, Matthew 5: 5 (King James Version).

While New Jersey Sleeps
Written at the time of the Camp David Summit between Israel and the Palestinian Authority (July, 2000).

Oh Lord open thou my lips/ And my mouth shall declare thy praise comes from the *Amidah* (Standing Prayer) which is central to Jewish liturgy. Sins are listed in the *Al Chet* (For the sin of…) prayer which is said ten times in the *Yom Kippur* (Day of Atonement) services. In some communities it is customary for people to beat their chests gently as each sin is called out.

Smothered prayer
Atticus…said you never really know a man until you stand in his shoes and walk around in them, To Kill a Mockingbird, Harper Lee, (London: William Heinemann, 1960).

Auden's Dog
Quotation from, *Musée des Beaux Arts*, The Collected Poetry of W. H. Auden, (New York: Random House, 1945).

Heat
For *eye for eye* see Exodus 21:24; for the story of Goliath see 1 Samuel 17; and for the story of Judith see the Apocrypha of the Old Testament.

June – November 2006
Israel-Lebanon War

A *wadi* is a valley.

Despondency
Israel-Gaza War, November 2012

July – August 2014
Israel-Gaza War

Batmitzvah (feminine) and *Barmitzvah* (masculine) is a rite of passage after which children are considered responsible for their own actions and may participate in all religious obligations.

Part 4: *The Fragmented Weight of Wanting*
During Balthazzar's Feast in Babylon, the words *MENE MENE TEKEL UPHARSIN* suddenly appear on a wall in the banqueting hall. Daniel is summoned to interpret the prophecy: *Mene, God hath numbered thy kingdom, and brought it to an end. Tekel, thou art weighed in the balances, and art found wanting. Peres, thy kingdom is divided and given to the Medes and Persians.* Daniel 5 (Soncino Press Version)

Unatoned 2
Isaiah 11: 6-9 (Soncino Press Version)
And the wolf shall dwell with the lamb, and the leopard shall lie down with the kid; and the calf and the young lion and the fatling together; and a little child shall lead them.

Unatoned 3
Ezekiel 37, specifically line 4 (Soncino Press Version)
Then He said unto me: 'Prophesy over these bones, and say unto them: O ye dry bones, hear the word of the Lord'.

Unatoned 4
The unifying theme of the Festival of Passover is blessing the escape from slavery and telling the story to each subsequent generation. The traditional text read during the celebratory meal, the *Haggadah* (Hebrew for 'telling' or 'saga'), presents Four Children, usually referred to as 'wise', 'wicked', 'simple' and 'the one who does not know how to ask', who reflect the challenges of transmitting knowledge and keeping it relevant. This part of the evening often generates discussions about freedom both historically and in contemporary times.

Garden Ruminations 1
Genesis 1: 27 (King James Version)
'So God created man in His own image, in the image of God created He him; male and female created He them.'

William Shakespeare, Othello, Act 3, scene 3: 301-304
If I do prove her haggard / Though that her jesses were my dear heartstrings / I'd whistle her off and let her down the wind / To prey at fortune.

Garden Ruminations 2
Isaiah 42: 6-7 (Soncino Press Version)
I the Lord have called thee in righteousness, and have taken hold thy hand, and kept thee, and set thee for a covenant of the people, for a light of the nations; to open the blind eyes, to bring out the prisoners from the dungeon, and them that sit in darkness out of the prison-house.

There are numerous verses in the Old Testament in which the Children of Israel are commanded to protect the vulnerable in

society characterised as widows, orphans and strangers. See for example, Leviticus 19: 33-34 (Soncino Press Version)
And if a stranger sojourn with thee in your land, ye shall not do him wrong. The stranger that sojourneth with you shall be unto you as one home-born among you, and thou shalt love him as thyself; for ye were strangers in the land of Egypt.

Garden Ruminations 3
According to Hassidic tradition, every night the soul stands on God's palm in order to reflect upon the day before being returned to the body (probably inspired by *Modeh Ani*, the morning prayer for waking up).

Garden Ruminations 4
See Genesis 2-4, for the Garden of Eden and Cain and Abel.

Threads 1
According to legend, Canute, the eleventh century king of England, Demark and Norway, is believed to have tried, unsuccessfully, to hold back the tide in order to demonstrate the power of God to his court.

Threads 5
The poem refers to the end of Samson's life. (Judges 16).

Backwards/Forwards
I will lift up mine eyes unto the hills, from whence cometh my help. Psalm 121 (King James Version).

BIOGRAPHY – SIMON LICHMAN

Simon Lichman, born in London in 1951, has lived in Jerusalem since 1971. He completed a B.A. Hons. in English Literature at the Hebrew University of Jerusalem, Israel (1975) and a Ph. D. in Folklore, The Gardener's Story and What Came Next: A Contextual Analysis of the Marshfield Paper Boys' Mumming Tradition, at the University of Pennsylvania, U.S.A. (1981). He is the founding Executive Director of the Centre for Creativity in Education and Cultural Heritage (CCECH), a non-profit-making organisation in Jerusalem, which brings together Jewish and Arab (Moslem and Christian) communities through education programmes based on folklore.

Simon Lichman has taught English Literature, Drama, Creative Writing, Folklore, Multicultural and Shared-Society Education, in Israel at the Hebrew University of Jerusalem, Ben Gurion University of the Negev (Beersheva), Kaye Academic College (Beersheva) and Tel Aviv University; at Knox College (Galesburg, Illinois, U.S.A.) where he was the Joseph B. Glossberg Visiting Israeli Scholar in 2011; and in England at Trinity and All Saints Colleges, Horsforth (1976-1978). He has regularly guest-lectured and given Master Classes in Poetry at the Juilliard School for Performing Arts (New York), Ohio State University (Columbus, Ohio) and Oberlin College (Oberlin, Ohio) in the United States of America.

He has published numerous articles about ritual drama and on the application of folklore to multicultural and shared-society education.

Simon Lichman has served as the Chairman of the Israel Association of Writers in English (IAWE), editing a number of issues of its journal, arc. His published poetry includes: Snatched Days (Elmer Press) and The Punished Wound (Palewell Press); and also appears in journals and anthologies such as arc, Ars Poetica, Can You Hear the People Sing? (Palewell Press),

Crosscurrents (New Zealand), European Judaism, the Journal of the American Geriatrics Society (JAGS), Konch, Modern Poetry in Translation, Stand, Tikkun, and Tri-Quarterly. He is currently working on two collections of poetry: The Harrowing, focussing on his family's Holocaust experience; and Entertaining Angels, after 'masterpiece' paintings of Biblical scenes.

Contact: simonlichman@yahoo.com

PALEWELL PRESS

Palewell Press is an independent publisher handling poetry, fiction and non-fiction with a focus on books that foster Justice, Equality and Sustainability.

The Editor can be reached on enquiries@palewellpress.co.uk

www.ingramcontent.com/pod-product-compliance
Lightning Source LLC
Chambersburg PA
CBHW050308120526
44590CB00016B/2535